Spot the Difference

Mouths

Daniel Nunn

Heinemann
LIBRARY

www.heinemann.co.uk/library
Visit our website to find out more information about **Heinemann Library** books.

To order:
 Phone 44 (0) 1865 888066
 Send a fax to 44 (0) 1865 314091
 Visit the Heinemann Bookshop at www.heinemann.co.uk/library to browse our catalogue and order online.

First published in Great Britain by Heinemann Library, Halley Court, Jordan Hill, Oxford OX2 8EJ, part of Harcourt Education. Heinemann is a registered trademark of Harcourt Education Ltd.

Editorial: Tracey Crawford, Cassie Mayer, Dan Nunn, and Sarah Chappelow
Design: Jo Hinton-Malivoire
Picture Research: Erica Newbery
Production: Duncan Gilbert

Originated by RMW
Printed and bound in China by South China Printing Company

10 digit ISBN 0 431 18239 1
13 digit ISBN 978 0 431 18239 1

11 10 09 08 07
10 9 8 7 6 5 4 3 2 1

British Library Cataloguing in Publication Data
Nunn, Daniel
Mouths. - (Spot the difference)
1.Mouth - Juvenile literature 2.Voice - Juvenile literature
3.Ingestion - Juvenile literature 4.Respiration - Juvenile literature
I.Title
573.3'5
A full catalogue record for this book is available from the British Library.

Acknowledgements
The publishers would like to thank the following for permission to reproduce photographs: Alamy p. **6** (Alaska Stock LLC); Corbis pp. **5** (Gary W Carter), **9** (Tom Brakefield), **12** (Amos Nachoum), **14** (Joe McDonald), **15** (Steve Kaufman), **18** (Zefa/Bach); FLPA p. **17** (Minden Pictures/Mitsuaki Iwago); Getty Images pp. **13** (Lonely Planet Image/David Tipling), **16** (Photodisc Green/John Giustina), **19** (Photodisc Green/Dick Luria), **21** (The Image Bank/Peter Dazeley); Harcourt Education/Tudor Photography p. **7**; Nature Picture Library pp. **4** (Pete Oxford), **8** (Anup Shah), **10** (Jane Burton), **11** (Tony Heald), **20** (Vincent Munier).

Cover photograph of a hippopotamus's mouth reproduced with permission of Steve Bloom.

Every effort has been made to contact copyright holders of any material reproduced in this book. Any omissions will be rectified in subsequent printings if notice is given to the publishers.

Contents

What is a mouth? 4

Different mouths 8

Amazing mouths 14

Your mouth 20

Can you remember? 22

Picture glossary 23

Index 24

What is a mouth?

mouth

Why do animals have a mouth?

Animals use their mouth to eat.

Animals use their mouth to breathe air.

Animals' mouths are
on their head.

Different mouths

Mouths come in many
shapes and sizes.

This is a tiger.
It has a big mouth.

mouth

This is a sea horse.
It has a small mouth.

This is a crocodile.
It has a long mouth.
Can you spot the difference?

This is a shark.
It has a wide mouth.

This is a woodpecker.
It has a sharp mouth.

Amazing mouths

This is a pelican.
It uses its mouth to scoop up fish.

This is a lion.
It uses its mouth to carry its cub.
Can you spot the difference?

15

This is a dog.
It uses its mouth to play.

tongue

This is a giraffe.
It uses its mouth to pull
leaves off trees.

17

tongue

This is a frog.
It uses its mouth to catch food.

teeth

This is a beaver.
It uses its mouth to cut down trees.

Your mouth

People have a mouth, too.
Like animals, people use their
mouth to breathe air.

People use their mouth to eat.

Can you remember?

Which animal's mouth is wide?
Which animal uses its mouth to
catch food?

Picture glossary

 **breathe** to take in air

 **scoop** to lift something up like you do when using a spoon

 **sharp** able to cut into something

Index

beaver 19

crocodile 11

dog 16

frog 18

giraffe 17

lion 15

pelican 14

sea horse 10

shark 12

tiger 9

woodpecker 13

Notes to parents and teachers

Before reading

Talk about how we use our mouths to eat and breathe. Tell the children to put their hands on their ribs, breathe in through their nose and feel their ribcages expand. Tell them to breathe out through their mouths and feel their ribcage contract.

After reading

Prepare slices of lime, a glass of tonic water, a bowl of salted crisps, and a bowl of brown sugar. Talk to the children about the four different tastes (bitter, sour, salty, and sweet) and allow them to try each taste in turn. Which do they like?

Draw simple face outlines and ask the children to make one mouth smiling and one mouth sad. Talk about when we are happy and sad.

Teach the children the following rhyme: "A wonderful bird is the pelican. Its mouth can hold more than its belly can!" (based on a limerick by Dixon Lanier Merritt).

Titles in the *Spot the Difference* series include:

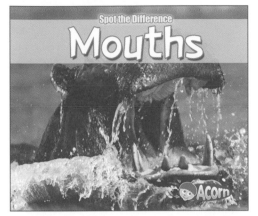

Hardback   0 431 18239 6

Hardback   0 431 18238 8

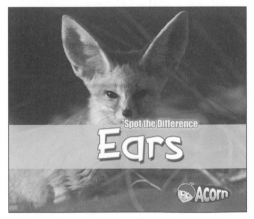

Hardback   0 431 18237 X

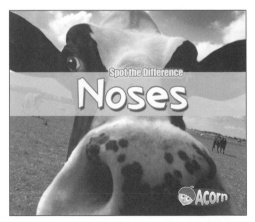

Hardback   0 431 18236 1

Find out about other titles from Heinemann Library on our website www.heinemann.co.uk/library